ONLINE VEHICLE

MERCHANDISING

THE FIRST STEP IN MODERN AUTOMOTIVE SALES

DENNIS GALBRAITH

DEDICATION

FOR THE MEMORY OF MY GRANDFATHER, JIM GALBRAITH (1908-1988), WHO BROUGHT HONESTY AND INTEGRITY TO HIS PROFESSION AS A CAR DEALER.

JIM GALBRAITH WAS RAISED IN THE MOUNTAINS OF THE MISSOURI OZARKS, IN THE SMALL COMMUNITY OF MOUNTAIN VIEW. TRUE TO HIS ROOTS, THE CHARACTERISTICS OF HONESTY AND INTEGRITY WERE NOT SEEN AS A MEANS OF PRIDEFUL DIFFERENTIATION; THEY WERE EXPECTATIONS ANY DECENT MAN HAD OF HIMSELF FROM CRADLE TO GRAVE.

ONE OF MY FAVORITE STORIES REGARDING MY GRANDFATHER INVOLVES BOTH HIS STUBBORNNESS AND INTEGRITY. HIS CHRYSLER-DESOTO DEALERSHIP IN COLONY, KANSAS WAS NOT ONLY THE TOWN'S DEALERSHIP BUT ITS REPAIR CENTER AND GAS STATION DURING THE 1950S. WHILE ONE OF HIS CUSTOMERS WAS HAVING THEIR TANK FILLED, SOME OF THE GAS SPILLED ONTO THE GROUND -- A FAIRLY COMMON OCCURRENCE EVEN WHEN I WAS PUMPING GAS IN THE 1970S. IF THE SPILL WAS SIGNIFICANT, A CENT OR TWO MIGHT BE DEDUCTED FROM THE PURCHASE, BUT ONE CUSTOMER INSISTED THAT AN ENTIRE GALLON HAD BEEN SPILLED ON THE GROUND.

MY GRANDFATHER'S FEELING WAS THAT HE COULD NEITHER AFFORD A REPUTATION FOR BEING SOFT ON SUCH AN OBVIOUS ATTEMPT TO TAKE ADVANTAGE OF HIM, NOR COULD HE RISK BEING PERCEIVED AS UNFAIR TO A CUSTOMER. HIS STUBBORNNESS KICKED IN AND HE POURED AN ENTIRE GALLON OF GAS ONTO THE GROUND IN FRONT OF THE CUSTOMER, "NOW THAT WE KNOW WHAT A GALLON LOOKS LIKE, LET'S REACH AN AGREEMENT."

DURING MY LIFETIME, MY GRANDFATHER RAN A SMALL STORE IN LANCASTER, CA. HE KNEW CARS, BUT HE KNEW PEOPLE EVEN BETTER.

HE HELPED ME UNDERSTAND THAT AUTOMOTIVE RETAIL IS LESS ABOUT THE VEHICLES THAN IT IS THE LIVES OF THE PEOPLE ENHANCED BY THOSE VEHICLES.

JIM GALBRAITH DID NOT LIVE TO SEE THE INTERNET'S IMPACT ON HIS INDUSTRY, BUT HE WELL UNDERSTOOD THE IMPORTANCE OF TRANSPARENCY AND REPUTATION MANAGEMENT. HE WOULD HAVE APPRECIATED THE INTERNET'S ABILITY TO ENHANCE THE SALES PROCESS IN BOTH THESE AREAS.

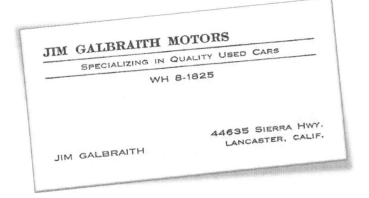

ACKNOWLEDGEMENTS

MANY THANKS TO THE COUNTLESS DEALERS AND VENDORS WHO HAVE BEEN SO GRACIOUS WITH THEIR TIME AND KNOWLEDGE OVER THESE MANY YEARS.

THANKS FOR ALL THE SUPPORT AND ENCOURAGEMENT FROM MY BOSS, JARED HAMILTON, AND THE TEAM AT DRIVINGSALES.

SPECIAL THANKS TO ALL THOSE WHO CONTRIBUTED PHOTOS AND INFORMATION:

- LINDA ADAMS AND HER TEAM AT CDMDATA
- GLEN GARVIN, JENNIFER RYAN, AND THEIR TEAM AT DEALER SPECIALTIES
- ALLAN CHELL AND HIS TEAM AT CDEMO.

DEEP APPRECIATION TO OUR DAUGHTER-IN-LAW, JENNIFER RENNO, FOR AGREEING TO MODEL FOR US AND FOR PUTTING TOGETHER THE COVER DESIGN.

NEVER ENDING GRATITUDE FOR MY WIFE, KATHY, FOR ALL HER LOVE, HELP, AND PATIENCE.

Contents

Introduction

Dealers of used cars and trucks are value added retailers, which means they are in the business of producing used vehicles. Dealers can't just buy a vehicle and slap a for-sale sign on it. There are mandated inspections to deal with, vehicle detailing, reconditioning, and merchandising. Producing used vehicles for sale is a production operation, and any other manager of production would recognize throughput as a key metric. Yet vehicles often wait idly for days or even weeks before they are ready for sale. In the age of transparency to the consumer, dealers cannot focus solely on the retail activities within the store. As a value-added retailer, enhancing value during the online sales process must become a core competency of the firm.

It can take just 20 hours to produce a new automobile on an assembly line. Yet the time it takes to get a used vehicle prepared and merchandised for sale is often 7 or 8 times that long. Manufacturers recognize that idle inventory is waste. They strive to reduce inventory stock to the fewest hours of required supply. We must accept that a used vehicle is simply a component of production, work-in-process inventory, until it is merchandised online. For the vast majority of shoppers, online is where they first see the vehicle they will purchase. Those vehicles not fully merchandised online with photos, video, and text descriptions are frequently passed over for those that are.

Grocers recognize their produce is useless in the warehouse, on the truck, or in the back room of the supermarket. Every effort is made to get fresh produce in front of customers as fast as possible. A case of produce can decline in value at a rate of dollars per day. Market analysis shows that the declining value of a used vehicle can also be measured in dollars per day, yet the same degree of urgency is rarely applied.

Speed to market is but one of the issues tackled in this book. The tone is deliberately blunt and to the point. Many millions of dollars are being lost every day, not just from publicly held corporations but from family businesses. At some point economic waste has got to come from someone's discretionary spending, a birthday or holiday gift, summer vacation, or a college fund. When that isn't enough to wake businesses up, it starts coming off the dinner table or out of the utility bill. Several decades ago, I put myself through the University of Southern California's prestigious graduate school of business by shutting off the gas meters of homes and businesses that could not pay their bills. I've caused thousands of children to go to bed cold and wake up to a cold breakfast and a cold shower. I've caused hundreds of restaurants, cleaners, and even factories to shut down in an instant. Darn right I'm blunt. I strongly prefer to wake business owners up before it's too late.

Automotive retail is more competitive than ever, and recognizing the production aspects of value added retailing is not enough. Much of what has been regarded as advertising is actually selling. In my first book, Sales Integration, I pointed out that the sales process generally begins online. Shoppers interact with automotive apps and websites in a back-and-forth manner that is far more akin to selling than it is to the one-way, interruption advertising done on television, radio, print, and outdoor display space. In short, online automotive merchandising is the process of producing sales content. It must sell effectively and be produced in a timely and efficient manner.

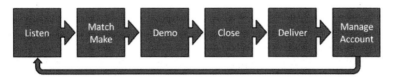

This graphic shows the sales process as I demonstrated it in my first book, Sales Integration. Online vehicle listings listen, match make, and begin demonstrating the vehicle; therefore, vehicle merchandising contributes more to selling than advertising.

This book is written for managers and owners. It scarcely skims the surface of the tactics and tools practitioners use to create effective vehicle merchandising in an efficient manner. It does, however, provide managers with the understanding and strategic thinking needed to oversee a successful merchandising operation.

To avoid reader fatigue, the book vacillates between talking directly to dealers and talking about them. The objective is to stimulate behavioral change among dealers resulting in greater profitability. Too much direct focus can produce an unintended feeling of being beat down. Therefore, the alternating from "your dealership" to "dealerships" attempts to avoid emotional fatigue due to style and allow for maximum emotional impact due to content.

Part 1, Increasing Sales

Chapter 1, Two Kinds of Preference

A CDM Service representative merchandising the vehicle with the iTab device. Photo courtesy of CDMData.

My grandfather owned the only car dealership in Colony, Kansas, a Chrysler/De Soto dealership. Many of his customers did not even own televisions. Customers often came by just to see what was available, but eventually he needed to establish enough preference for his vehicles and his store to keep shoppers from going elsewhere when it was time to buy.

Today, over 80% of shoppers begin their shopping process online. If preference for the vehicle and the store are not established online, chances are the dealership will never even know the shopper was in market. You win online, or you don't have an opportunity to win at the store. Every store has a base of loyal customers with enough preference for the store to give them consideration. But when it comes to generating sales from new customers, having a great team of closers in the store with a poor online presence is like gearing up for the playoffs and having a losing record in the regular season. You must win online first, or nothing else matters.

Some shoppers want a specific vehicle and are willing to travel hundreds of miles to get it. Other shoppers are loyal enough to consider every vehicle in your store before turning to another dealership. Most shoppers require a high level of preference for both the vehicle and the store before they even make the decision to step on the lot. Vehicle merchandising is not just about maximizing preference for the vehicle. The quality of your photos, videos, seller's notes, and vehicle condition reports say a great deal about the kind of store you operate. Transparency signals honesty. Accuracy and clarity signal professionalism.

Dealer Preference
• Reputation or Image
• Location
• Available Financing

and/or

Vehicle Preference
• Vehicle Type
• Make, Model, Trim, Options, Color
• Price

Contact with the Store

A complete set of photos helps the online shopper feel as though they understand the vehicle. It can also deliver the impression that the dealership is upfront and forthcoming. The right lighting for your vehicle photos makes the car more appealing to the shopper, and it sends a message about the professionalism of the dealership. Tiffany's does not just offer jewelry, their stores include dozens of attributes designed to add value to the jewelry. Many auto dealers do the same, but not all. For many shoppers, their first serious look at your store will occur only after they gain interest in one of your vehicle listings. They have no prior idea what your store looks like inside or how you operate it. The expectations of the shopper are formulated online. Unless the store appears professional in the way it merchandises it's vehicles online, the shopper may never see the store.

It is generally agreed that videos need not be studio quality to make a favorable impression about your store. However, the audio quality should be very good and the tone of voice must match the intended image of the store brand. The lighting must be void of bright reflections and other negative distractions that detract from the vehicle image.

Text descriptions with spelling errors and poor punctuation can dampen shoppers' perceptions of the store. Outlandish claims can cause damage to the store's credibility throughout the sales process. On the other hand, candor regarding the condition of used vehicles can dramatically alter shoppers' impressions of the store's honesty. Getting shoppers to view your dealership differently from stores they shopped previously can lead to higher close rates, bigger grosses, and more loyalty and advocacy from customers.

Chapter 2, Winning on the Search Results Page

The Search Results Page (SRP) is different across the various listings sites like AutoTrader.com, Cars.com, and CarSoup in the U.S. or Kijiji and AutoTrader Canada in Canada. However there are a number of common characteristics. Virtually all of them display the primary vehicle photo, the price, the mileage, and some information about the vehicle in text.

Listing from a Search Results Page (SRP) on Cars.com. Notice that the first vehicle is aided by the "Click for Specials" button that shows up as a bright green on the website. The second listing It is newer and has fewer miles but lacks any photo, inviting negative speculation and putting the vehicle at a considerable disadvantage.

The Primary Photo

The first thing actual vehicle photos help establish is that you actually have the vehicle. Other dealers have played a variety of games with inventory they did not have in a bait-and-switch effort to get shoppers into the store. Stock photographs do nothing to minimize these concerns. This is a key reason why shoppers of new vehicles select vehicles with actual photos far more often than those with stock photos or no photos. AutoTrader.com holds a great deal of data regarding the impact of various online merchandising, and their strong recommendation is to avoid stock photos altogether and particularly as the primary vehicle photo.

Related to this issue is equipment. Shoppers want to see the vehicle the way it actually appears, as equipped. Listing mistakes have been all too common. Sometimes the VIN decoding is inaccurate and sometimes equipment is added or removed. Shoppers want to see the vehicle as it really exists.

Listing from a Search Results Page (SRP) on AutoTrader.com. Note that the second vehicle is actually Sterling Gray Metallic, yet the stock photo is of a white truck. There is no indication what color the first vehicle is. The third vehicle is the only one the shopper can be certain is white.

For the primary photo, most dealers appear to be moving toward a 3/4 view of the vehicle showing the left-front corner. I've heard any number of trainers swear there is research to indicate this works best. Frankly, I was never able to prove the existence of this research and am doubtful of its existence. That said, I understand what stimulated the hypothesis and have no argument with it. Advertising expert David Ogilvy taught us long ago that the eye is drawn first to the picture. It makes sense that English and Spanish reading people will start with the photo in the listing and move to the right. I don't know of a single listings provider that does not put the photo on the left side of the listing. Those arguing for the left-front corner of the vehicle as the primary shot reason that it points the car in the same direction they want the eye to go, left to right. They want to minimize the chance that the eye will go down to the next listing instead. Now that you know the argument, feel free to choose for yourself, but the 3/4 view is certainly standard.

The front ¾ view has become the standard first photo. Photo courtesy of Dealer Specialties.

The more important issue is having a photo. Cars.com reports listings with a photo receive three times more Vehicle Detail Pages than listings with no photo. They certainly have enough data to know. The primary reason vehicles don't have photos is a poor merchandising process. Vehicles wait for days or even weeks before being photographed. The chart below shows the percentage of vehicles with no photos within various ages of the listing. Collectively, the data represents over 1.3 million listings as they appeared on Cars.com October 30, 2011. This snapshot in time shows that 94% of listings eventually receive photos, but fewer than half of them receive photos within the first three days and fewer than 60% within the first week.

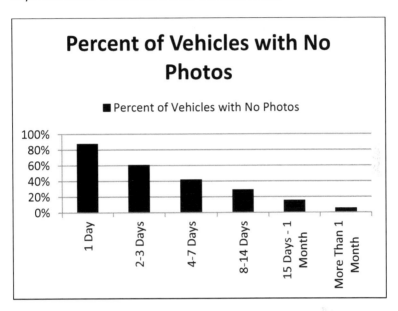

Since the same information is sent to other listings sites, it is fair to assume the results are similar for all listings. It has been argued that some photo feeds may lag behind the vehicle information coming from the Dealer Management System (DMS). This is not the case for all listings and cannot account for more than a one-day delay when the problem does exist. Clearly, the major problem lies in the process of getting out and taking photos of every vehicle the first day it is offered for sale.

The solution for this will be discussed in the Speed Through Simplicity chapter within the next section. What is essential to understand at this stage of the reading is the importance of eliminating this problem within your store through process.

Listings with photos convert from the SRP to VDP at least three times more than vehicles without photos. It can be said with little exaggeration that a vehicle without photos is virtually not for sale. The longer vehicles wait for photos, the slower the inventory will turn. It is just that simple. Show me two stores with the same used-vehicle inventory at the same prices in the same market and I assure you the one with the better process for rapidly merchandising their inventory will enjoy significantly better inventory turns. The difference is somewhat diminished for new vehicles, but the principle still applies.

Percieved Value
Price relative to mileage and age has a tremendous impact on the conversion from SRP to VDP. If value is defined as benefits divided by price, then it can be said that consumers often measure value by the remaining expected vehicle use divided by price. Perceived value generally goes up as the expected miles, age, and/or price go down.

Some vehicle features contribute mightily to the vehicles value, which is why listings providers have been adding more and more ways to filter the inventory over recent years. Cars.com and AutoTrader.com both make it possible to filter the consideration set by transmission, engine, 2WD or 4WD, number of doors, fuel type, and color. Cars.com exposes these filters on the SRP and AutoTrader.com exposes them prior to displaying the SRP. In both cases, these sites have ample inventory in most markets to display dozens or even hundreds of vehicles matching the shopper's criteria. Within these more tightly defined SRPs, shoppers are left to decide which vehicles they want to explore first based on the three primary value determinants - price, age, and mileage. Each of these variables are also filterable, leaving an even more defined consideration set of vehicles.

For new vehicles, mileage is not a value determinant, although the model year can be during transition periods where the outgoing model year is in stock while the incoming model year is being added to dealer inventories. When model year, features and color are equal or similar, the primary differential is the dealership itself. There is no difference in vehicle preference when vehicles are identical. Preference for the store becomes the primary factor determining which store receives the first call. Remember however that how vehicles are merchandised impacts preference for the store. Two identical vehicles are rarely identically merchandised. Actual photos, clear photos, videos with good tone of voice, and well constructed text descriptions can be all the differentiation one store needs over another in attracting the first call on an identical vehicle. In some cases, a small price differential can be more than overcome with by a strong merchandising differential.

In today's competitive market, it is absolutely essential that dealers know how each vehicle will stack up on the SRP in terms of value. Based on the year, make, model, and trim (YMMT), what are vehicles with similar mileage selling for? Any dealer can look at the transparent market place in real time and know how their vehicle will stack up. Of course, that would be a painful amount of work for dealers buying and selling dozens of vehicles every week and often having to reevaluate them multiple times prior to sale.

Dale Pollak recognized the need for a Software As a Service (SAS) solution to this problem. One that would cost less to use each month than either the improvement in profitability created by the information or the cost of generating it manually. His creation was vAuto, and he artfully articulated the benefits of using the product to fulfill the velocity strategy outlined in his books and presentations. Alternative solutions like FirstLook and DealerTrack's aax also took root.

Regardless of which tool a dealership purchases, it is useless until utilized. I have yet to analyze a dealer's used-vehicle inventory without finding multiple areas of potential improvement. Given the rapid rate of valuation changes in some segments, some minor imperfections should probably be expected, but many stores have ridiculously inappropriate pricing. It is common to find both some vehicles ridiculously underpriced given the scarcity of supply relative to demand and other vehicles ridiculously overpriced in light of market conditions. These simultaneous differences are not a result of pricing tools or pricing strategy. They are a result of the tools not being used or not being used properly.

Owners cannot simply purchase these tools and assume the issue is handled. My own view is that the providers of these products are shortchanging themselves by convincing dealers that a periodic call from one of their analysts will set everything straight. It doesn't work, and the result is hundreds of dealers swearing up and down that the products or the strategies don't work, when in fact dealers are simply not working them.

Proper pricing requires education, discipline, and a lot of hard work. I ranked among the top 1% in the nation for mathematics on my college entrance exams and the top 4% on my graduate school entrance exams. I understand math and logic, and I'm telling you anyone who thinks this stuff is simple does not understand the full depth of it. The demand for employees with solid math skills is growing faster than our national education system has any chance of keeping up with. Dealerships don't generally attract a lot of quant types to begin with, so this problem is bad now and sure to get worse in the future.

Many stores will find they need to hire a pricing or price advisory team serving a multitude of non-competing stores to aid in this work. Dealer groups will increasingly recognize the need to centralize pricing in order to provide the kind of scale necessary to justify the required level of talent. For GMs, this is going to go over like a turd in the punch bowl. To many, the inability to set price at the store level is justification for resignation. Nonetheless, store level pricing authority has disappeared from supermarkets, department stores, home improvement stores, bank branches, chain restaurants, and on and on. It can happen in automotive retail as well.

The optimal solution is for pricing tools to become easier to use. On the vendor side, many product managers overly focus on the development of new features. Having run a large product team for three years, I fully understand the attraction for feature-focused development. However, making these tools easier to use is what dealers truly need from vendors. There is value in making these decisions at the store level, but the labor force does not exist today that can work the existing tools to the desired results with the training currently in place across 17,000 franchised stores. Every aspect of this situation, from tools to training to the willingness to be guided by facts rather than gut feel must evolve quickly.

Auto dealerships are Main Street's last businesses of significant size attempting to making product, pricing, and promotions decisions at the store level. Be prepared to understand and use the analytical tools at the store level or risk having them made for you by a centralized team.

Text Description

As mentioned previously, the importance of the brief text description within the SRP varies from site to site. On sites like AutoTrader.com, this information stands out on the page, and the number of characters shown has been expanded over the years. This vital real estate must be used to do one or more of the following:

1. Highlight the features, options, and accessories that add value and differentiate the vehicle
2. Demonstrate price difference or superior pricing policy
3. Enhance preference for the store

The following pages show actual text descriptions of vehicles found on Search Result Pages from AutoTrader.com. The right way to approach text descriptions depends on the vehicle type, the vehicle price relative to competitive offerings, the dealership and its position in the market, and state regulations for advertising.

The opening line of this text description is rock solid, but it shouldn't be the opening line. If your store has a haggle-free policy, or any other policies appealing to shoppers, let that be known. However, this should be accompanied with text demonstrating that the price shown represents a fantastic value. After all, the other vehicles on the page can also be purchased at those listed prices without haggling and those dealers may even be willing to come down on their price.

Consider demonstrating value at the offered price, then letting the shopper know you always have to post great prices online because you are a no-haggle store.

MSRP $61910 Retail Customer Cash $2000 Promo Bonus Cash $1000 Ford Credit Cash $1000 Brien Discount $4955 Total Discount $8955. This vehicle has a 6.7L V8 OHV 16V DIESEL engine and an automatic transmission. It includes Sliding Rear Pickup Truck ... View more details

This vehicle was listed for $52,955. Immediately showing that the MSRP was nearly $8,955 higher gives a quick sense of value. This discount is the summation of four individual discounts, which must be disclosed. The vehicle runs on diesel. It is vital that this attribute be clearly listed. Getting a click on this listing from a shopper looking for a gasoline engine does you no good.

For those shoppers looking specifically for diesel, you want to be able to stand out.

Shoppers can query results by fuel type on both Cars.com and AutoTrader.com. Although most shoppers do not take advantage of this feature, those looking for a specific fuel type have considerably narrowed their options. By making sure your vehicle is properly listed, you assure its inclusion in these specialized search results. If the dominance of gasoline as a fuel type slowly declines over time, the number of these fuel-specific searches may increase.

> Vehicle price may include all available rebates including owner loyalty, $500 military rebate, and may require financing with a captive lender. Not all applicants or vehicle models will qualify for all available rebates. Please contact us prior to... View more details

This text description includes all the necessary disclosures and may lead some shoppers to conclusion they don't know what the real price is. There is nothing in this description to indicate the price is a significant value. By default, most SRPs list vehicles in price order, so the vehicle is going to be flanked by similarly price vehicles. The question the shopper needs answered is whether or not the vehicle is a good value at that price.

> Nothing feels or drives like a new vehicle. If you don't see what you want, give us a call, and we will get it! At ███. we work for you!

The name of the dealership has been redacted from the above

listing. This is a trickle-poor excuse for a vehicle description. There is nothing here that could not be said about any other vehicle at this or any other store. Most major listings sites have 2-3 million vehicles listed. The sites are designed so if you don't see what you want you just keep looking on the site until you do.

FEATURES and OPTIONS This vehicle comes equipped with AM-FM, Leather Interior Surface,, CONTACT US

The contact information has been deleted from this listing. It is doubtful that the existence of an AM-FM radio is the most distinguishing feature on this vehicle. Other features that generally don't need to be seen on the listing within the SRP for new or late-model used vehicles are:

- Power windows
- Power locks
- Intermittent windshield wipers
- ABS brakes
- Power brakes
- Clock
- Heater
- Trip odometer

Features that should be considered as highlights on the SRP include:

- Heated seats
- 3rd row seats (when only two rows is possible)
- Club cab or extended cab on pickup trucks

27

- Diesel/Hybrid/Electric
- Handicap equipped

OEM Certification

One of the advantages of OEM certification on used vehicles is the inclusion of that brand's Certified Pre-Owned (CPO) logo on the SRP. If the shopper filters the results to show only certified vehicles, then only those vehicles listed with the manufacture will be display. When the shopper selects all used vehicles, the CPO designation makes the listing stand out.

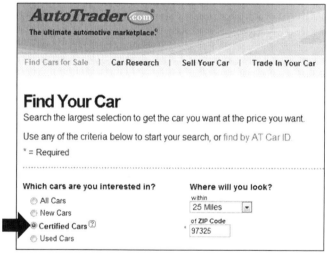

When the "Certified Cars" option is selected, only manufacturer certified vehicles will be shown on the SRP.

The certification designation helps the listing stand out against non-certified vehicles.

Whether the shopper is looking only for certified vehicles or considering them among a broad list of used vehicles, the manufacturer CPO designation is a huge plus on the SRP. Having this designation will generally result in more VDPs per 100 SRPs than would otherwise be the case.

Manufacturers spend a considerable sum of money to make sure their certified vehicles receive a competitive advantage on listings sites. They typically provide listings services like Cars.com and AutoTrader.com with daily feeds of those vehicles that are registered with the manufacturer as certified. Certification programs have performed very well for most luxury brands and their dealers. While analyzing the data on certification programs for J.D. Power and Associates, I found, not surprisingly, that consumers tend to place more value on certification for higher priced vehicles.

Dealerships selling non-luxury brands often find the manufacturer's CPO program beneficial for 1-3 year old vehicles and models in high price ranges. The fact is that virtually every luxury brand has one or more models starting at under $35,000 and many non-luxury brands offer vehicles selling for more than $50,000 when nicely equipped. Certification may not be as important to a Nissan dealer whose used inventory is focused on vehicles under $20,000. However, a dealer serving a market that can appreciate late model 370Zs, Murano CrossCabriolets,

Armadas, and nicely equipped Titans should strongly consider the advantages of manufacturer certification.

Other Distinguishing Logos and Designations

AutoTrader.com allows the dealership's logo to appear on the SRP. Since every dealer can have a logo, the trick is to make your logo stand out. If you have a robust branding campaign that features your logo, then using the identical version of the logo will help your listings stand out as a recognized brand. However, if you have not invested in a strong branding campaign for an extended period of time, consider going with a logo version that will standout on the page. While neither of the logos below are wonderful, the logo for Crown Ford does not stand out nearly as well as the logo for Fayetteville Auto Marts.

NEWLY LISTED

Used 2007 Ford F150 4x4 XLT

* 80,327 miles • Black

-PRICED BELOW THE MARKET AVERAGE!- -NEW ARRIVAL- -POPULAR COLOR!- PRICED TO SELL AT $19,441 WHICH IS $3,657 BELOW THE MARKET AVERAGE! This Black 2007 Ford F-150 is priced to sell and has 80,327 miles . This F-150 won't last long so be sure to ca... View more details

$19,441

📷 21 Photos

9 miles from ZIP code 28348

Crown Ford

1-866-765-3169

▸ http://fayettevilleford.com
▸ New Ford's up to 40% off.wow!!

View our inventory

Used 2008 Ford F150 2WD Sup

* 74,266 miles • White Sand Metallic

4.6L V8 EFI. Talk about a deal! The truck you've always wanted! Tired of the same uninteresting drive? Well change up things with this reliable 2008 Ford F-150. New Car Test Drive said it "...delivers a combination of style, interior comfort,... View more details

$17,726

📷 27 Photos

9 miles from ZIP code 28348

Fayetteville Auto Marts

1-877-786-0564

View our inventory

The dealership logo should match the branding of the store, and should be designed to help the listing stand out.

The logo is hyperlinked to the specials page for that dealership, yet there is nothing to indicate that. In the example above, Crown Ford is attempting to encourage clicks to the specials page by including the word "Specials." Some stores have gone as far as using "click here" as their logo. At this time, there is no known research isolating the impact of the logo design on clicks from the listing or clicks from the logo itself. Undoubtedly, a logo tied to a brand recognized by consumers and representing a compelling Unique Selling Proposition (UPS) will increase the SRP to VDP conversion rate.

If your brand fits this description, then the primary objective for the logo design should be brand recognition. Absent a strong branding campaign for the logo to be associated with, the primary objective should be to help the listing stand out with color and design, but within the parameters of the vehicle category. A neon green logo probably isn't a good way to stand out on a page of listings for $70,000 luxury vehicles.

AutoTrader.com also provides the linked logo for free CARFAX reports when offered by the dealership. Cars.com provides a small, undistinguished link for the same purpose. The linked logo for AutoTrader.com's own Trade-in Marketplace is also included in listing from dealers participating in the program.

Cars.com includes a brightly colored link to either new-car specials or used-car specials when those programs are subscribed to. It has been my experience after plowing through a great deal of listings data that virtually any logo or enhanced designation will generate slightly more clicks than an otherwise equally competitive listing without such distinction. These upsell features do result in higher conversion rates from SRP to VDP.

The differences between listings providers is less important than making your listings stand out relative to others on the same page. Marketers do need to make quantitative decisions regarding which listings services to invest in. Once those decisions are made, the more important activity is figuring out how to make each individual marketing investment pay off best. These are participatory models, and that participation needs to be worked in every detail for maximum competitive advantage.

Investment decisions must also be made on up-sell and related products associated with the primary investment of posting listings. From a purely strategic perspective, it makes more sense to stock OEM-certified vehicles if you are advertising on those sites giving preference to them. Providing free CARFAX reports is worth more to you if you advertise on sites that promote that fact. Investing is specials products generally makes more sense for dealers with a large enough inventory to offer a multitude of closely related vehicle alternatives. From what vehicles are stocked to how to price and merchandise them, none of these decisions can be made in isolation of the others.

Filterable Features

Certification is not the only vehicle feature that can be filtered for by the shopper. Transmission, drivetrain, fuel type, and door count are all filterable features from the SRP on Cars.com and on the advanced search section on AutoTrader.com. CarSoup.com also has advanced search capability, allowing the shopper to sort by engine, transmission, fuel type, drivetrain, and whether or not the vehicle is handicap equipped. Unfortunately, many vehicles are listed as "unknown" for one or more of these features. When shoppers filter for pickup trucks with two doors or four, thousands of the listings on Cars.com are ineligible as "unknown."

Just running the VIN exploder is no longer sufficient. These key, filterable items must be present. Most shoppers do not use these filters, but those who do are looking for something specific. What a tragedy it is when you have what the customer is looking for, yet your vehicle is eliminated from their consideration set because that information is not listed online. Chances are the customer will never see your vehicle or come into your store.

Getting the information for used vehicles correct requires an inspection process that is simple enough that anyone could do it quickly. That generally means recording the inspection as the photos are taken, guided by the same device. The Mobile Inspector application is designed to make sure this information is collected during the merchandising process and recorded on the same device. Initially, this added responsibility can slow down the merchandising process, but this is temporary. In my field observations of the product in use by seasoned merchandisers, this additional task quickly becomes absorbed as part of the process with little additional effort.

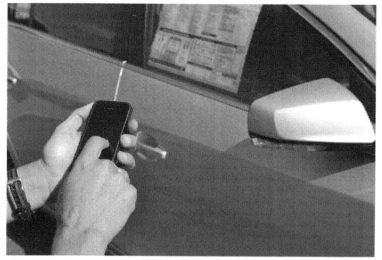

Using the iPhone app, Mobile Inspector, by cDemo to verify vehicle attributes while taking photos and recording video.

Tiered Listings

Some services show listings to consumers in tiers. AutoTrader.com is the largest of these examples. Buying your way into a higher tier will give your inventory more exposure. There is no question about this. Upgrading AutoTrader.com listings from Featured to Premium or Premium to Alpha will absolutely result in more VDPs, more contacts, and more sales. With three months worth of data, the results should be obvious and measurable. The trick is knowing whether the additional boost in traffic is worth the additional cost, or whether those marketing dollars would be better placed somewhere else.

The only objective for moving listings higher on the SRP is to receive more VDPs. Therefore the proper analysis is the marginal cost per VDP. By dividing the change in cost by the change in VDPs, we know the marginal cost per VDP. It is then possible to compare the cost per VDP achieved from various product levels when listings are tiered. We have already seen multiple things that can increase the conversion from SRP to VDP whether the listings are in a higher tier or not. In some cases, those applications may be more cost effective than buying up to a higher tier.

$$\frac{\text{Change in Cost}}{\text{Change in VDPs}} = \text{Marginal Cost Per VDP}$$

Acceptable Cost Per VDP

The objective from the SRP is to maximize the number of VDP generated at the most cost effective rate possible. Cost per VDP is the most reasonable metric for measuring performance toward this objective. How well the vehicle is merchandised on the SRP has a significant impact on the rate at which SRPs convert to VDP, yet price is the single largest variable contributing to this rate. Maximizing total gross requires market oriented pricing combined with great merchandising to demonstrate superior value.

The acceptable cost per VDP varies from store to store. Those stores with better merchandised vehicles on their VDPs will receive better conversion from VDP to phone, email, chat, or walk-in traffic. Therefore, they can afford to pay more per VDP. This is critical for the many upgrade products like AutoTrader.com's Premium and Alpha or Cars.com's Premier product. The dealers with the most applicable inventory and best merchandised inventory can afford to pay more for these services than those dealerships with fewer applicable vehicles and/or less persuasive merchandising.

> *"You'd be hard pressed to find a dealership that sells more than 100 used retail without generating at least 10,000 VDPs."*
>
> *– Dale Pollack on DalePollack.com, September 2011*

A higher rate per VDP might be acceptable to one dealership than to another due to differences in back-end gross. Doing a fantastic job of earning money on the back end – in the F&I stage – makes it possible to justify a more aggressive advertising spend to acquire front-end opportunities. It is very difficult to make more on the front end of a sale than the market will bear. However, there is ample opportunity to make additional profit on the back-end, with the right training and mix of products. This fact was initially brought to my attention by my friend Tony Volpe, VP at Continental Warranty. The 2011 paper he inspired me to write and Continental Warranty sponsored, *The Profit Filled Back-End of Velocity*, demonstrated the fantastic opportunity available to dealers who "price for show and work the back end for dough."

Chapter 3, Converting from the Vehicle Details Page

The vehicle detail page (VDP) is where the shopper starts interacting with the content you provided about a specific vehicle. From here, it doesn't matter what your average number of photos are, only whether the photos on that page sufficiently build preference for the vehicle and the store. The same can be said for the quantity of videos or the length of the seller's notes. Quality is what truly matters, and the quantity of content necessary to deliver the complete message varies from vehicle to vehicle and store to store.

Vehicle Detail Pages are not necessarily the same from one website to another. However, the content fed to them generally is. Chances are, your store has a feed sending information out to every site you wish to expose your inventory on. Conversion from SRP to VDP may vary from site to site for a variety of reasons, but conversion for a specific vehicle on any site is largely a function of the price, market forces, and the content about the vehicle and store found on the VDP. If you placed two identical vehicles on a website with the same pricing but different merchandising content (photos, videos, text descriptions, history report, and condition report), the one with the best merchandising may not receive any more VDPs, but more of those VDPs will convert into a phone call, email, chat, or walk-in customer.

The more shoppers you expose your inventory to, the more important your merchandising is. This is true online just as it would be on a busy street. If traffic patterns shifted and your frontline vehicles suddenly received twice as much exposure to drivers passing by, then the appearance of your store from the street would become twice as important. As you think about adding new listings sites to your promotions, also consider improving your merchandising. As you improve your merchandising, also consider exposing it more shoppers on your website or others. In 2011, I began referring to this as the seesaw effect.

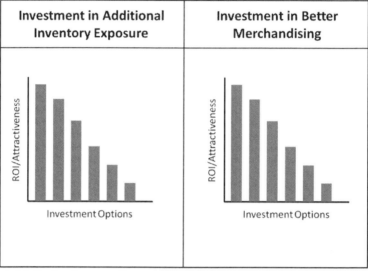

Initially, both sets of investment alternatives may appear the same.

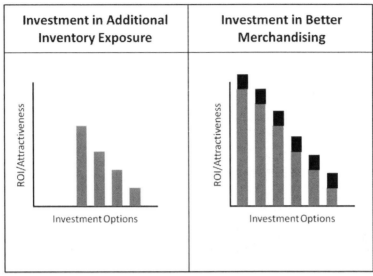

As more money is invested in exposing the inventory, the return from every merchandizing option is enhanced.

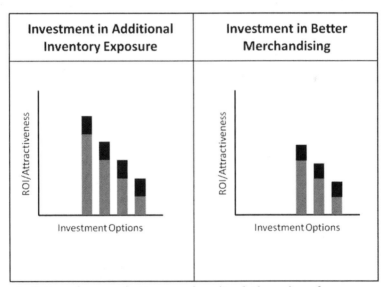

As listings become better merchandised, the value of additional exposure is enhanced.

We find seesaws all through marketing, which is why it is impossible to optimize the marketing mix as a specialist. You can't optimize results by doing only that which you want to do or only following the advice of a few specialists. This book is about online vehicle merchandising, but it is essential to put that effort into the context of the overall marketing.

Vendors tend to have a bias for their product, and that is to be expected. Those vendors who are worth seeking the advice of view the market holistically. They often recognize that proper advice about your promotions today will likely enhance the value of their offering tomorrow. Those who are laser focused on today's sales are not worth spending much time with.

This chapter covers each area of merchandising content impacting the conversion from VDP to contact. The proper way to compare the cost effectiveness of improving each is by measuring the marginal cost per contact. This may be different from store to store. By estimating the value of each contact (phone call, email, chat, or walk-in) we can compare the value of efforts in Chapter 3 aimed at turning more VDPs into contacts with those in Chapter 2 aimed at turning more SRPs into VDPs. We can even compare both to the option of lowering price to improve both forms of conversion.

Photos

As mentioned previously, the primary photo helps the shopper know that you actually have the vehicle and what it looks like as equipped. Stock photography cannot provide these reassurances. The vehicle's photo gallery should build on this level of disclosure. Interior, exterior, and under the hood are all photo areas that demonstrate to the customer what benefits the vehicle has to offer relative to its price.

It is foolhardy to assume all shoppers are capable of translating text descriptions of vehicle features and options into visualized benefits. Photos help bring these benefits to life. Arguably, video can do an even better job of this, but many people shop at work or in other locations where turning the sound on may not be an option. Therefore, photos will always be a critical part of merchandising new vehicles.

The most common argument against fully demonstrating new vehicles with photographs goes something like this, "So I show the shoppers what the color-coordinated carpet with King Ranch mats look like on this F-150 and they know what they look like in every other dealer's King Ranch version, all effort and no gain." My answer to this is twofold:

1. They found the information while looking at your vehicle from your store.
2. There are 10 different F-150s, and many shoppers know all too well that a significant number of Ford salespeople can't articulate the differences. Your site indicates you can.

For used vehicles, photos are the key to establishing credibility. In some cases, photos of imperfections are more important than the photos suggesting nothing is wrong on that portion of the vehicle. There is nothing you can photograph that the customer won't be able to see for themselves once they are in the store. For many shoppers, providing full disclosure upfront eases their concerns about the reliability of the powertrain and other areas of the vehicle they can't judge for themselves.

A quality photo helps the shopper feel they understand the vehicle, but it does more than that. A good photo with a clean background and clean flooring says something about the kind of store you run and the way the shopper can expect to be treated. Many generations ago, it was said that you couldn't expect a horse trader to treat you any better than he treats his horses. That same general feeling is shared by many skeptical shoppers. Before you decide whether to have a dedicated location for studio-quality photography, ask yourself whether your store is more like Nordstrom or Dollar Store. If you are trying to extract a premium for the level of your service, your photos are your first chance to signal to the customer what kind of store your are operating.

Lighting is the most difficult part of creating quality photos. This is the key advantage of having a dedicated, indoor location. Without control of the lighting, the vehicle often needs to be turned several times to prevent unwanted glare or reflections. A tent or other structure may be able to block the light from above as well as the south, southwest, and southeast. At a minimum, you'll want to block out direct sunlight for 180 degrees. This may or may not provide sufficient natural lighting. Chances are you will need to supplement your dedicated photo area with a proper lighting kit.

All this may seem excessive, but a look at the numbers suggests otherwise. Look at the price you are currently paying per contact (phone, email, chat, and walk-in). Then calculate how many more contacts you would need to justify the monthly depreciation and utilities associated with a dedicated photo bay or facility. Also factor in the improved efficiency of not having to move the vehicle around. You may find that this investment is one of the most cost-effective things you can do. However, the most important reason for a controlled environment is that the job gets done every day. The vehicle is virtually not for sale until it is merchandised online. If you are losing even one day per vehicle because of weather or poor lighting during the only time someone is available, then you are losing two sales per month for every 100 vehicles in stock (assumes a 50-day average inventory turnover rate).

It is important to photograph the vehicle from a variety of distances. The exterior styling of a vehicle is generally judged from a distance. Inspection for scratches, dings, and smudges requires a closer look.

The photos in this section are not designed to show all the shots recommended for each vehicle type. The intent is to show why some of the most common photos are important to shoppers. Understand the objectives, and you can use your creative talent to meet those objectives in a way that gives your store a competitive advantage.

Profile pictures and other distant shots are necessary to demonstrate the image of the vehicle. Photo courtesy of Mobile Inspector by cDemo.

It may seem excessive to take a variety of front-end pictures, but drivers know this is where damage often occurs from rocks and other objects. Add the most close-up detail where wear is expected. Photos courtesy of Mobile Inspector by cDemo.

How low can you go? Many shoppers don't get down this low to inspect the vehicle, nor should they need to. Win trust by informing shoppers about the things they may not even think to check for. Photo courtesy of Dealer Specialties.

Bring transparency to the areas most susceptible to wear and stain. Photo courtesy of Mobile Inspector by cDemo.

Get close up on the places frequently touched. The dirt and wear in these places are some of the signals to shoppers that it's time to trade their own vehicles. Your vehicle with less wear and better detailing may give them the perception of regained status and less risk of vehicle failure. Photos courtesy of Mobile Inspector by cDemo.

Do vehicles run better after they've been washed? Many people perceive that they do. It's just natural. There are so many things about modern vehicles that shoppers cannot judge the remaining life of. Entire systems are a mystery to many shoppers. They many never have seen a heater core or a crankshaft. They may not know a power steering unit from an air conditioning compressor, and they darn sure don't know how to inspect these things. What they rely on is the timeless notion that things that are clean and show less wear on the outside last longer on the inside. Great detailing combined with close-up photos are a surefire way of demonstrating value.

The value of great detailing extends to the engine compartment as well. Photo courtesy of Mobile Inspector by cDemo.

The information in these photos can and must be explained in text form as well, but photos add credibility. Shoppers generally believe what they see more than what they hear or read. Photos courtesy of Mobile Inspector by cDemo.

This is a better view of the remaining tire tread than the shopper is likely to obtain while in the store, transparency at its finest. Photo courtesy of Mobile Inspector by cDemo.

If the wear pattern shows slight signs of alignment, balance, or inflation problems, replace the tire or be transparent about the problem. Let the shopper know the problem has been fixed. Faking transparency can damage credibility in an irreparable way.

My old friend, Ralph Ebersole, taught me that using a coin in the picture could demonstrate the depth of the tread in a photograph.

When merchandising vehicles with cDemo CEO, Allan Chell, he handed me a gauge for measuring the remaining tread depth. He also showed me how to use that measurement to estimate the remaining tread for the vehicle condition report. People like Allan, with many years of experience, can often look at a tire and estimate the tread depth within a 32nd of an inch or within a millimeter. For the rest of use, the gauge is a quick source of accuracy for the vehicle condition report. However, it is difficult to photograph a standard gauge in a way that makes the tiny markings visible, and Allan advised against it. While the photograph below demonstrates the measurement taking place, it's hard for many shoppers to put that into context.

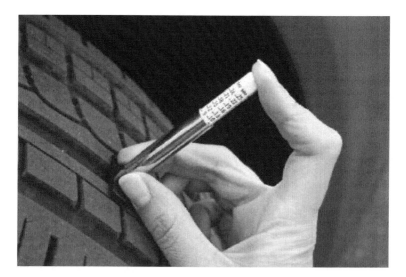

Turning the front tires all the way takes a few extra seconds in the production process, but it allows the merchandiser to take a good, clean shot of the tread.

Photos of the cargo area are vital for vans, SUVs, and wagons. Most people shopping for these vehicles are not attracted to them by their stylish appearance. They have things that need to travel with them. Don't assume the shopper understands the versatility of the vehicle. Show the features that allow shoppers to hang shopping bags or safely retain tall or heavy loads.

When I was running the Automotive Internet department of J.D. Power and Associates, I presented the results of the Manufacturer Website Evaluation Study to nearly every OEM twice each year. One of my recommendations for photographing the trunk space of compact cars was to include bags of groceries, golf bags, or some other item that would help the shopper realize just how much space was available. Kia was one of the first to use this method but many manufacturers followed. If it is available, this is one bit of stock photography that is recommended as part of your photo gallery.

When photographing the cargo area, demonstrate the amount of space, the versitility, and the condition of the vehicle. Photo courtesy of Dealer Specialties.

Videos

About 25% of the public are auditory learners. It's not that they don't learn from what they see and do, but they don't get as much from those senses as most of us do and usually get more from what they hear than visual or kinesthetic learners do. For these shoppers, video is of extreme importance. Everything else about your listings are visual, and invite the shopper to come experience the vehicle (kinesthetic). Video adds to the visual experience by adding motion and backs that up with audio. Those shoppers who don't read the book and wait for the movie are very glad to see you meeting their needs with video.

Many services exist that can make a video from your still photos and seller's notes. Your description of the vehicle becomes the audio track, and the images are animated to simulate moving pictures. This is an economical way to go, and even this kind of stitched video from stills with a computer voice is better than no video at all. However, using the voice of an actual person has fantastic benefits. This is your one chance to connect with auditory learners. Additionally, the information being heard may appear more reliable. If the person doing the talking is actually with the vehicle as they are talking, there is a better chance of establishing credibility regarding the vehicles features and conditions.

Text is easily misunderstood, but audio adds information and feeling beyond the raw meaning of the words. There is not yet any solid research on the best type of voice for live video recording. In my opinion, sincerity rules. I'd rather have someone doing the video who is genuinely excited for the next owner of the vehicle than someone with a radio quality voice that is just verbally listing the vehicle's features.

The video does not necessarily need to cover anything new. Remember the old motto of professional speakers and teachers: tell them what you're going to tell them, tell them, then tell them what you told them. Some shoppers will only utilize their preferred method of communication. Some shoppers will take in the same information in text, photo, and video form. That's okay. Before spending tens of thousands of dollars on a vehicle, it's best to know it inside and out. More information is generally much more excusable than too little information.

Other shoppers will simply go directly to the form of media they absorb information from most or easiest. If you do not give shoppers access to video, some will be forced to absorb your vehicle information your way or go to another vehicle from another dealership. Remember that the shopper is still online. You probably don't even know they are in market, and your competitors are only one or two clicks away.

Modern vehicles have more interior motion than was ever dreamed of years ago. Seats don't just lean down, they fold over, flip up, fold flat, or even come out of the vehicle altogether with the push of a button. The ease with which this happens has gone through fantastic advances over recent years. Don't assume all your shoppers understand this. You may be selling an SUV to someone who never owned one before. Use the motion aspect of video to demonstrate ease of use, something you just can't do with text or photos.

The fact that more is said in this book regarding photos and text than video is purely a function of the fact that it is difficult to explain video in a printed medium. The relative brevity is no reflection on the proportion importance of video. Looking forward, I expect video to become even more important to online automotive merchandising over time.

Text Descriptions

The internet has moved from primarily a text medium in its early years to a multimedia platform. Bandwidth improvements have allowed more emphasis on richer forms of communication, like photos and video. However, good text descriptions remain important to converting shoppers from the VDP into store contacts via phone, chat, email, and walk-in traffic.

Although most stores provided shoppers with some form of text description for a decade or more, some basic rules remain unheeded. Your listings should not be in all capital letters or include sentences or phrases in all caps. Text is easily misunderstood. In response, Internet users found ways of injecting emotion into their text that goes beyond that which is conveyed in the words. One of these techniques is to use all capital letters to signify shouting or yelling. Generally speaking, this is not your intention. Dealers using all capital letters often do so to signify excitement. However, the expression of excitement is best left to exclamation marks, and not too many at that.

All CAPITAL LETTERS in text today is similar to *fortissimo possibile (fff)* in music dynamics. The difference is a volume increase in music is more easily interpreted and put into context. Volume in a product description is just interpreted as yelling by many shoppers.

My good friends Joe Webb and Bill Playford are trainers with a fantastic use of humor in their work. They did a fine job of mocking the importance of listing every vehicle feature in one of their popular YouTube videos. The fact is, even if every vehicle of a particular year/make/model has ABS brakes and intermittent windshield wipers some shoppers don't know that. In some cases, although not most, your vehicle may be at a disadvantage by not listing these features.

It makes sense to separate the differentiating features from the common ones. Those features that differentiate the vehicle form others of that make/model are the features that should be elaborated on and mentioned early in the text description. This is the case for both new and used vehicles. Make it obvious that your vehicle is a superior value. If a used vehicle is a one-owner vehicle, that information should be cited early on in the text description.

The merchandising of new vehicles is generally poor across the internet. While weak arguments can be made for stock photography, no plausible argument can be made against fully utilizing text on the VDP to enhance preference for the store. There is a good chance some other dealer has a white Camry with the same equipment yours has. What differentiates new vehicles from commodity products is the difference in the value added by the retailer.

The differences between your store and others are largely the same regardless of the new vehicle being sold. This presents and ideal opportunity to create one masterpiece statement than can be posted on every VDP on your website and used as the batch tagline for your listings on third-party sites. Explain the why-buy-here difference on the VDP or accept the fact that you are going to lose sales to dealers who do.

Vehicle History Report

Providing a Vehicle History Report (VHR) says as much about your store as it does about the vehicle itself. If you offer a free VHR on your used vehicles, then let that be known on the VDP. Including a few highlights from the VHR in the text description of the vehicle can further add to the credibility of your store, particularly if something negative is disclosed and mitigated.

Which VHR is best depends on shopper recognition within your region. CARFAX is a very strong brand name, but is not universally acclaimed across all markets. If another product is stronger in your market, then don't be afraid to use it. However, CARFAX is strong enough that those answering phone calls, chats, emails, and handling walk-in traffic will need to know how to explain why you use something other than CARFAX when challenged on it.

Most vehicle certification programs include a VHR as part of the standard offering. If the manufacturer's certification program enjoys high penetration rates in the market – most of the vehicles that can be certified are certified – then using the VHR brand specified for certification is generally the best bet for both certified and non-certified vehicles.

Vehicle Certification

Manufacturer certification programs remain the most respected certification programs and are often the only programs recognized by independent listing sites. The primary promotional difference is how the vehicle is merchandised on the SRP. On the VDP, it is your responsibility to highlight the fact that the vehicle is certified, regardless of what type of certification program is utilized. Chances are, the shopper is unaware of the features of the certification program. Listing those program features can help differentiate your vehicle from those that are not certified or covered by an alternative program.

For most certification programs, the vehicle must be registered with the manufacturer as certified in order for it to show up as certified on listing services. Frequently, that means the vehicle is going to need to be priced a bit higher than it would be without the certification attached.

By the time the shopper gets to the VDP, you have their attention in the vehicle even at the higher price. However, you are going to have to demonstrate the benefits of the program to those who do not fully understand it, which includes the majority of used-vehicle shoppers. Failure to sell the certification benefits on the VDP can easily cost you the sale to a dealership selling a comparable non-certified vehicle.

Vehicle certification remains more a function of supply than of demand. I've studied this category since 2000 and saw early evidence of this fact and it continues on today. More and more people have a vague understanding of manufacture certification programs, but what determines how many certified vehicles of a given brand will be sold in a quarter is almost entirely a function of how many certifiable vehicles dealers of that brand purchase and how many of those they choose to certify. I'm constantly amazed at the trade reports of brand X going up or down in its certified sales with no indication of whether that is a higher or lower percentage of the certifiable vehicles coming into the market. When a large number of vehicles are coming off lease at the same time, certified sales should be expected to rise. When there is a dearth of certifiable product coming into the market, sales are bound to go down.

What dealers, manufacturers, and trade publications should all be focused on are the percentage of certifiable vehicles being certified, the speed at which certified vehicles sell, and the gross profit from certified vehicles. Ultimately, it is the turn rate and profit margins associated with certified vehicles that will get more dealers into the certification program and actively bidding on certifiable vehicles.

Vehicle certification is the most complex intangible product car dealerships have ever tried to sell through frontline sales people. I developed that explanation when consulting with the CPO teams at GM, Chrysler, BMW, and others back in 2003. It is as true today as it was then. Understanding this, helps dealers understand why they need to do everything they can to explain the certification program online. Doing so reduces the risk that the opportunity will be lost online and reduces the risk that it will be blown at the store. Most CPO buyers learn the details of the program at the store, yet few stores can boast having a complete team of salespeople who can adequately explain the program. Certification gives your listing an edge in being seen and selected on the SRP. Fully explaining the program on the VDP helps keep your vehicle in the consideration set and better positions the store for success when handling the customer.

At the peak of my involvement with CPO programs (2003-2006) there was ample evidence that certified vehicles were turning faster and receiving higher gross profits. The most convincing evidence of this came from the Power Information Network. As I worked with GM, Audi, and Subaru to educate their dealers on marketing certification in 2008 and 2009, the data I was then receiving second hand bore the same indications. Nonetheless, this experience of faster turn and higher grosses was not universal across all stores. Certification programs work, but you must look at your Vehicle Detail Pages and your sales team as you ask yourself how well you are working the certification program.

Vehicle Condition Report

Although the inclusion of a Vehicle Condition Report (VCR) is commonplace for online wholesale auctions, the practice is just beginning to take hold in the retail market. As more and more consumers expand their shopping radius, the desire for a VCR prior to visiting the store or purchasing sight-unseen will increase. At least one store is now seeing as many as 20% of the sales that go through the BDC closed by the BDC with no need for a floor appointment other than signing docs and picking up keys. This is achieved with a substantial VCR.

At the first J.D. Power Internet Roundtable in 2005, I pointed out the importance of disclosing all detectable flaws online. A small scratch or tear may decrease the value of the vehicle $25 or more, but the added credibility that comes from fully disclosing it upfront may earn your store a premium over competing stores, regardless of which vehicle is purchased.

The presence of a vehicle condition report provides assurance that the vehicle was inspected. It is one thing to disclose any flaws in the vehicle, but transparency around what was inspected provides a much higher level of shopper confidence. It stands to reason that if vehicle condition reports are allowing more shoppers to confidently purchase the vehicle sight-unseen, then those shoppers coming to the store for a vehicle they reviewed the VCR for online are likely coming in with more confidence and a higher propensity to buy.

The Mobile Inspector application from cDemo has been used in Canada for several years. It provides the option of producing a vehicle condition report while collecting photos and creating a live video. Combining these three production processes appears to be the most efficient means of production, and the app makes it simple to do.

Any process for producing a VCR must include a device that guides the user, rather than a user guiding the device. Following a process on paper is simply not efficient enough, and memorization of processes applicable to all vehicle types is simply not realistic given the low volumes of most stores and wide range of used vehicles carried. Could someone get good enough at producing VCRs to do so without the aid of a guiding application? Sure, but then what happens when that person is sick, on vacation, or takes a day off? The vehicles wait until the one expert returns to perform the task. As noted earlier, time is the reason 17% of vehicles listed online do not even include a single photo. How much more difficult will it be to include a VCR with every vehicle if your store is reliant on an expert skill set.

By including the process in the software or application, the required skill level is dramatically reduced. This allows for quick and easy replacement of personnel, whether lost on a temporary or permanent basis.

The inclusion of a Vehicle Condition Report from the VDP will be one of the biggest changes to used-vehicle sales over this decade. Pricing transparency is useless, if not misleading, unless the price is tied to a vehicle listing that is as complete and transparent about the product as possible. Over the next few years, there will be a rapid increase in the number of VCRs conducted by dealers for their retail sales and by private citizens in an effort to maximize the value of their vehicle for private-party sale or as a potential trade-in.

Already, stories are commenting about shoppers using the Mobile Inspector app to solicit trade-in offers from various dealers. Increasingly, shoppers are selling their vehicles without obligation to buy one in exchange. The success of CarMax's buying program greatly benefited its wholesale auction business. According to the firm's 2011 annual report, the wholesale auctions were up 33% in unit sales and topped $1 billion in revenue. If consumer generated VCRs are incorporated into the program, they may be able to pull business in from an even greater distance.

The CarMax program is clearly a threat to dealers, but the rapidly expanding CarBuyCo is not. The firm does not sell vehicles at a retail level, so there is no threat that the dealer will lose the sale as well as the trade. Fundamentally, there is growing competition for the acquisition of used vehicles from consumers, and consumer generated VCRs are bound to be a growing part of it. It would be unreasonable to expect consumers to begin creating their own VCRs, complete with photos and video, and not expect at least as much from the dealers they are considering buying from.

The natural evolution of product transparency, combined with ease of production, increased shopping distance, and the growing use of consumer generated VCRs all points in the same direction. Get ready to include the production of VCRs alongside photos, videos, and text descriptions in your used-vehicle merchandising.

Financing

The primary consumer benefit promoted and delivered by some stores is vehicle financing, rather than the vehicle itself. That is appropriate in some markets, and it impacts the pricing strategy of those stores. As long as dealers are able to increase the acceptability of finance applications by manipulating price and trade-in value, there will always be some dealers who price high in order to provide the maximum flexibility for financing.

Most buy-here-pay-here stores do not list their inventory on sites like AutoTrader.com and Cars.com. Due to the nature of their business, they cannot afford to post market competitive prices. To some degree, the price varies based on the risk associated with the financing. Posting a market-competitive price puts all the risk premium into the interest rate, which then appears usurious. This is why buy-here-pay-here stores often do not post price on the vehicles.

The pricing constraints may not be as extreme for franchised dealers as they are for buy-here-pay-here dealers, but they are serious enough to keep many stores from listing price. For these stores, listing vehicles on AutoTrader.com, Cars.com, and other sites may or may not pencil out. However, they will need to list their inventory on their own site at a minimum. Since the dealer is not focused on price, the listing must emphasize that the dealer has special financing capability.

For these shoppers, the best deal is not the one with the lowest price, it is the one they can qualify for. The easy financing message is probably what got the shopper to the site in the first place. Emphasize it on the VDP to increase conversion from this page to a phone, chat, email, or walk-in contact. The importance of this emphasis is so great that A/B testing should be conducted to see which approach maximizes the number of tracked contacts (phone + email + chat) per VDP.

Trade-In Policy

Virtually every store takes vehicles in trade, but the processes for doing so have become increasingly diverse over the past few years. AutoTrader.com has its Trade-In Marketplace, moving a large portion of the trade-in process online. CarMax has its own process for evaluating trades online. As previously mentioned, CarBuyCo adds another dynamic to the market.

With online competition growing for the customer's trade-in, it is more important than ever to disclose your trade-in policy on the VDP. With the exception of CarBuyCo.com, the sites competing for your customers' trade-ins are also competing for the sale. You can't afford the risk that the shopper will leave your VDP to start looking for the best trade-in option. There is a good chance that shopper will not be back to your listing, regardless of their intent when they left it.

The VDP cannot be fully transparent unless it provides all the information related to the complete transaction. There has been a great deal of complaining and moaning about a race to the bottom on vehicle prices, yet those who complain the loudest are often the most guilty of not fully utilizing the VDP to explain why the shopper should choose them as the next place to call, email, chat, or walk into. The trade-in policy is one of the many things that contribute to full transparency on the VDP. The dealer not offering the lowest price can point to the fact that they are not just pricing low to get the customer in and skin them on everything else. Done properly, the complete candor may significantly elevate preference for the store.

Chapter 4, Facilitating Decision Making *In Absentia*

Regardless of what may appear on the registration, most vehicles are not purchased by a single person functioning alone. Most vehicle shopping is done by a pair of decision-makers or a decision-maker and a strong influencer. Generally speaking, people feel most comfortable recommending something they feel like they really know. A vehicle only half merchandised leaves many unanswered questions, making it awkward to send that vehicle to another person. For many shoppers, it is more natural to simply mark the vehicle as one that needs more information, possibly a phone call or a chat with the dealership. But the reality is, that action often does not take place. The shopper keeps looking online for an equally attractive option that is fully merchandised.

When it comes to making joint decisions, we generally don't like to have our recommendations second guessed. We particularly hate getting pinned down with questions we don't have answers to. Many dealers have asked me, "Dennis, shouldn't I hold some information back to make the customer contact me?" My answer is always "Heck no!" There is a good chance that the next contact is not with a dealer, but with the other decision-maker. The other decision-maker may even feel slighted if he or she finds out a dealer has been contacted before consulting them. Complete merchandising is essential for facilitating decision making when you can't be present.

Your merchandising mission is not simply to inspire contact with the store, it is to inspire advocacy of your store and vehicle from one person to the other. Virtually every salesperson has lost a deal where one decision-maker was in favor of it but the other was not. Getting the customer to come in more ready to buy starts with getting both decision-makers seeing eye to eye before they even come into the store. One or both decision-makers may even be worried about exhibiting a fracture in their relationship at the store. Avoiding this kind of embarrassment requires going to the store with as few potential surprises as possible.

Utilizing the internet for joint decision making is not limited to shopping for a vehicle. "What do you think about this for Robert's birthday gift?" "What do you think about this for our holiday card?" "I really like this necklace." These are things shoppers used to discuss with catalogs in hand on the family sofa or at the dining table. Now they are happening online. Shoppers send each other links, and increasingly they look at things together over tablets.

Tablets are portable, yet big enough to share. They allow decision-makers to share information and see the reaction of their partner. The facial expressions communicated from one person to another are lost with link sharing, but not with tablets. Fully 30% of the time a table computer is used is while watching TV. Another 21% of tablet computer use takes place in bed. (Data on horizontal vs. vertical use is not available, but is a request I hear often.) The first test of your vehicle merchandising is often not whether it will drive the customer to contact the store but whether it will drive the decision-maker or influencer to move your vehicle into the unified consideration set for serious discussion.

Those shoppers who do contact the dealership to gather additional information for discussion with their partner are often a waste of time for dealership personnel. How much of what you tell the customer will be remembered? How much will they share with the other person? How much will they get wrong as they make the next link in the daisy chain? How much will the other person assume they heard wrong? When your vehicle's complete story is front and center in text, photos, and video, both parties are not only getting the same information, they are confident that they are. The likelihood of disagreement or embarrassment at the store is minimized, and confidence about moving the shopping process toward the store is enhanced.

Chapter 5, Speed to Market

The only thing positive about finished goods inventory is the opportunity for gross profit. Therefore, it stands to reason that maximizing the ratio of gross profit/inventory is an essential objective for dealers. Of course, if we can turn inventory more rapidly, our preference would be to scale that operation, increasing inventory and increasing gross profit even more. The classic argument is whether the dealer should price to maximize gross profit per unit or price for the fastest inventory turn, making up the difference with volume. The good news is that price is not the only area responsible for the inventory turn rate. If you can improve the rate at which your vehicles sell without lowering the price, then you have a real winner. Let's call these non-price velocity enhancers.

In fact, it doesn't matter how low you price your inventory online, it isn't going to sell quickly until it receives at least a minimal level of merchandising. I can post a 2009 Honda Civic at 85% of the average market price, but if it doesn't have any photos, video, or a good description, it won't get a lot of traffic. The speed with which you bring new inventory to market fully merchandised plays a big role in how fast your inventory will sell and how much gross profit you can make from you current inventory level.

When Bill Pearson, GM of Finish Line Ford, said "If the vehicle is not online it's not for sale" it was not much of an exaggeration. The corollary to this is that if it is not fully merchandised online it is not fully up for sale. That is to say, it is available to consumers, but we haven't given them any reason to include the vehicle in their consideration set.

At many stores, the gap between the Sales Department and the Service Department is so wide that Sales simply accepts the rate at which Service reconditions and details vehicles. The simple fact is that you cannot turn your inventory every 30 days if it spends the first six in Service and waits another three days before it gets fully merchandised. Savvy dealers are unifying their stores to become factories for the rapid production, merchandising, and sales of used vehicles. The same could be said of new vehicles, minus the need for reconditioning.

In any other production process, we would recognize three distinct categories of inventory:

- Raw materials - components for making a product
- Work in process (WIP) - components already in the process of becoming a product
- Finished goods - products ready for sale

In some states, vehicles cannot be advertised for sale until they have completed the state vehicle certification process. When this is the case, inventory should be broken down into the categories above.

- A vehicle is categorized as Raw Materials Inventory from the time it has been purchased until the process of reconditioning and certification has begun.
- Once the process of getting the vehicle ready for sales has begun, it is classified as WIP inventory until it is posted for sale.
- From the time it is posted for sale to the date it is sold, the vehicle is listed as Finished Goods Inventory.

Getting vehicles into and through the production process quickly is vital to efficiency. No revenue can be obtained from

Raw Materials or WIP inventory. From this perspective, we want finished goods to be the highest possible percentage of total inventory. On the other hand, this ratio can also be inflated by an inability to quickly sell the Finished Goods inventory. Maintaining an average of 95% Finished Goods inventory and only 5% Raw Materials plus WIP might seem sufficient. However, this ratio is much more impressive for a store turning its inventory every 30 days than for a store turning its inventory every 60 days.

Typically, dealers combine these two terms by looking at the average number of days it takes to bring the vehicle to a finished-goods state. When it comes to improving (lessening) the time it takes to produce finished goods, it is helpful to understand where the bottlenecks are. There are a number of reasons why vehicles might linger in a Raw Materials state.

1. The acquisition process delivers vehicles in large batches, producing a backlog of inventory waiting to enter the process
2. The amount of process work per vehicle is not consistent
3. The capacity of the production process is not consistent

Those involved in the production process often feel they are most efficient when they have an ample supply of Raw Materials. Downtime due to a lack of Raw Materials can appear inefficient. However, it may be less efficient to maintain a backlog of vehicles to be reconditioned and certified than it is to have occasional periods of idle production capacity. Balancing the two is essential.

Those involved in acquiring vehicles may be able to achieve a lower Cost to Market average by procuring vehicles with a wide range of reconditioning needs. However, consistent throughput time requires consistent inputs into the process. The optimal balance between bargain hunting and process efficiency is something that must be identified for each store.

Waiting for Pricing

In many states, it is permissible to advertise vehicles even before they have been reconditioned. This is a practice that should be done where possible. The argument about not being able to price the vehicle until reconditioning is complete represents a complete failure to understanding the science behind pricing.

Cost have nothing to do with pricing. Whether a store's policy is to market vehicles with a fixed price, a price that leaves some room for negotiation, or a price that leaves a great deal of room for negotiation, the cost of the vehicle has no bearing on what that price should be. Market forces of supply and demand are the only determinants of pricing. The supply portion of this relates to how many other vehicles exist in the market and what the store's cost will be to replace the vehicle. Two identical vehicles in the same market, from the same store, at the same time should be priced the same. It does not matter whether one needed a new radiator and the other did not.

The customer expects the vehicle to have a functioning cooling system, and they are not going to pay a premium for one that just received a new radiator over one that did not. A recent cooling system repair is not a competitive advantage. If this kind of surprise occurs in the reconditioning, then the front-end gross will be impacted, but an adjustment to the offering price will likely only increase the length of time it takes to sell the vehicle, further hampering total gross for the store.

Reconditioning items that will impact the value of the vehicle (e.g. cosmetic repairs) are known to be needed at the time the vehicle is acquired. Those costs are factored in before the vehicle is even bid on. Reconditioning costs that cannot be factored in before bidding on the vehicle are generally not going to impact the vehicle's retail sales value. In short, the ability to immediately merchandise a vehicle online with the price should never be held up waiting for cost information.

Chapter 6, Improved Close Ratios

There are five ways in which shoppers transition from purely technological touchpoints to engaging someone at the store:

1. Phone
2. Email
3. Chat or Text
4. Video Chat
5. Walking In

The shopper gets to pick how the initial engagement is made and when it happens. Preparation and speed are essential in all cases. When handling phone calls, the representative must have all sites open, as well as the management system. If the customer is looking at a vehicle on an independent site, the rep must be able to instantly see that vehicle on that site to facilitate the best possible communication. If the customer is on the manufacturer's site, the rep must be able to instantly see what the customer is seeing. These same standards apply to chat, texting, or video chat. Every time a representative says "I'll get back to you on that" the sale is in jeopardy. Chances are the shopper will not be idly waiting for a return call. They will likely be searching across other options or contacting other dealers.

It begins to become clear that many shoppers are not transitioning completely from technological touchpoints online to a human touchpoint exclusively. In many cases they have not left the computer. They are simply adding the human touchpoint. Often, the purpose for contacting the store is to gain additional information or verify information found online. Unfortunately for many stores, the people answering the shoppers calls don't have good information, particularly with respect to used vehicles. Does the vehicle have heated seats?

The picture looks like an aftermarket audio system, is it? Does the SUV have a cargo net or any other accessories that were not standard on the vehicle? This information must be captured as part of the vehicle merchandising process in order for the representative to be able to provide timely and accurate answers.

One might argue if all that information is collected during the merchandising process, then it should be included in the online vehicle description. I could not agree more. However, just because it's there does not mean every shopper will find it. Most shoppers only go through this process every few years. Your reps make a living at it. There will be questions, and your reps will be able to answer them if the information is recorded as part of the vehicle merchandising process.

So how in the world does this happen? The things to look for vary by vehicle type, make, and model. Do you need someone with an extraordinary memory who knows exactly what to look for on each type of vehicle? When I was pumping gas at Mobile and Chevron stations in the 1970s, it was hard just learning where the gas tank and dip stick was for each type of vehicle. With all the various models and accessories on them, I can't imagine a single person being able to remember everything there is to look for. Fortunately, systems exist today that allow the device to drive the operator rather than the other way around. Smart phones are not just smart about phoning, they are smart cameras and smart information collectors as well. The app can tell the operator what to look for at each step of the process. This allows the operator to record any differences from the data brought in from the VIN explosion.

There are systems for capturing photos, systems for capturing photos and video, and systems for capturing photos, video, and detailed information about the vehicle. The latter is what some stores need for the merchandising process if they are to meet the needs of shoppers at the critical point of initial contact.

Whether you operate a BDC or handle all incoming contacts "cradle to grave," having complete and accurate information at the fingertips of your sales team will result in more appointments set and more appointments that show. When your team can provide quick and accurate answers, and be able to show the customer where it can be found online, that doesn't just answer their question about the vehicle it answers their question about what kind of store you operate. By now, most consumers over the age of thirty have a vehicle shopping experience where they or their shopping partner knew more about the vehicle after shopping online than the person trying to sell it to them. Often, shoppers call stores half expecting to not be able to get an answer to their question. Sometimes they leave the call unsure whether the answer they did receive was true. The way your people answer questions has a direct impact on their ability to set the kind of appointments that result in sales.

That same information found to be so critical in appointment setting is vital to floor sales as well. When I think back to some of the answers I gave shoppers when I was selling vehicles, I know darn well I would not get away with them today. Like most stores, we carried a great deal of used inventory from manufactures we were not franchised to sell. For many stores even the new inventory is difficult to keep straight. Ford currently carries 5 different cars, 5 different crossovers or SUVs, 5 different trucks. And that does not account for the 3 vehicles in hybrid version and 8 commercial offerings. It also doesn't account for the many different trims. The F-150 alone comes in 10 distinct versions.

Needless to say, it is getting difficult for salespeople to keep everything straight. Many stores are responding by putting tablet computers in the hands of their frontline sales people. This makes perfect sense to most shoppers. Just as a phone call or chat is often coming from someone while the shopper is looking at vehicle information online, walk-in customers often come into the store armed with smart phones. Shoppers used to go from purely technological touchpoints to purely human touchpoints when getting off the computer and coming into the store. That is often not the case today, especially among the shoppers who buy from franchised dealers. In 2011, the Pew Internet Project reported that 35% of adults carried smart phones. For new-vehicle buyers, that number has been reported to be as high as 80%. That may be inflated, and the number is surly a bit lower for buyers of certified and late-model used vehicles. Nonetheless, when tablets are included, it can safely be assumed that over half of all shoppers walking into a franchised dealer's store have instant access to the internet through some kind of device in their pocket or purse.

The problem with smart phones is that the small screen is not designed for sharing. Often, shoppers will wait for a moment when the salesperson is absent to check their phone for other options or to verify information. By putting an iPad or other tablet computer in the hands of your salesperson, they have the right information, and the information is credible. They can avoid be-backs by showing the customer how the value of your offering stacks up to the competition without leaving the lot.

In writing my first book, *Sales Integration*, I studied a wide variety of high-end durable goods sales. I am convinced that consumers will soon come to expect the people who sell cars, homes, boats, and power sports to be able to do so with tablet computers in hand. The presence of a tablet computer signals that the agent can provide detailed information quickly and demonstrate that the information she shares verbally is consistent with what is recorded in the system. The fly in the ointment is the old saying, garbage in garbage out. Yes your frontline people can enjoy higher close ratios and fewer be-backs walking off the lot, but it will require some work on the front end. Tablet computers work best in the sales process when the vehicle merchandising process is complete, not only providing photos and videos but confirming the text description of the vehicle and providing a vehicle condition report.

The chart below demonstrates the many ways consumers shop across multiple channels. The information about your vehicles must be consistent across every site they are listed on as well as in your store. Great sales integration starts with inputting complete and accurate information about the vehicle as soon as the vehicle is available for sale.

Multi-Channel Shopping

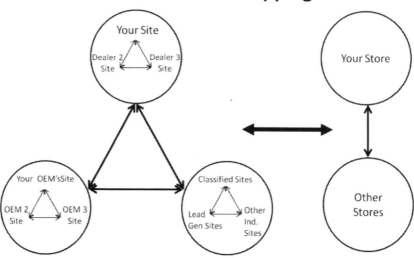

Part 2, The Production Process

Chapter 7 Speed Through Simplicity

Speed is essential to many areas of business, and it is particularly critical in retail. The faster vehicles get merchandised online, the sooner contacts start coming in from shoppers interested in those vehicles. Adding additional information. like vehicle condition reports, to the merchandising mix increases the need for streamlined processes. No matter how well your vehicles are merchandised online, some shoppers will not find what they are looking for or want assurance that it means what they think it does. The faster your team is able to provide that information, the fewer the number of sales lost. Lack of speed can cost a store business either by customers searching other offerings while waiting or abandoning the store for a more professional establishment.

As both a business owner and a corporate executive, I've found that knowing how to achieve speed is a huge competitive advantage. The auto industry itself was built on a process change for the purpose of gaining speed. The assembly line made it possible to build cars much faster. It did so by simplifying the tasks for each individual working on the line. In all my years of studying the ways to achieve speed and putting them in place, I've found simplicity to be the first vital step. Online merchandising is no different.

I've seen extraordinary production out of people who have been taking photos of vehicles for years. They get very good at it. But what happens when you want more from them. Maybe you want additional pictures for SUVs with third-row seating. Maybe you want to start adding pictures of the tire tread on used vehicles, or the odometer reading, or the VIN. Maybe you want them to start taking video as well, and verifying the features of the vehicle as well as the other elements of a vehicle condition report. People get fast by knowing their process. Change that process and you risk losing speed. Make a lot of process changes at one time, and speed is sure to suffer. However, if the process is built into the device (camera, smart phone, tablet computer) for the purpose of guiding the user, then you can change the process with less disruption to speed. When the user needs to learn how to handle the device differently to make a process change, speed is impacted. When the manager simply programs a different process into the device that guides the user, the impact on speed is diminished.

In the days of Henry Ford, speed was achieved by breaking a process down and assigning a limited number of steps to each person. This was based on the scientific management work of Frederick Taylor. Everything must be standardized. The more steps one person needs to be accountable for, the greater the risk to standardization.

Today we are able to build software that guides individuals through processes requiring far more steps than they could memorize and providing them with the ability to adapt on the fly. One clear example is navigation systems. Tell it where you want to go, and it guides you through all the steps needed to get there. Roads change over time, and updating the software is much simpler than updating a box of maps or the mind of the operator. How navigation systems work may be complicated, but they bring simplicity to the process of driving to new places.

Similarly, applications like Mobile Inspector guide the operator. Just as your car tells you how to operate it, the iPhone app tells you how to operate the iPhone to merchandise the vehicle.

Putting the VIN and desired level of merchandising into the app is similar to putting an address into a navigation system. It sets the destination (e.g. photos, video, and a detailed vehicle condition report for a 2008 Ford Explorer Limited).

Jennifer follows the process embedded in this iPhone.

Having one service that sends feeds directly to all the sites listing your inventory simplifies this part of the system. Many companies simplify this portion of the process by relaying the data from the dealership to the outside vendors requiring it. They send merchandising information directly to the cloud, where it then feeds all the systems listing the dealer's inventory, including the dealer's site and any internal systems. Minimizing the number of potential problem points is the kind of simplicity that can assure speed on a continual basis.

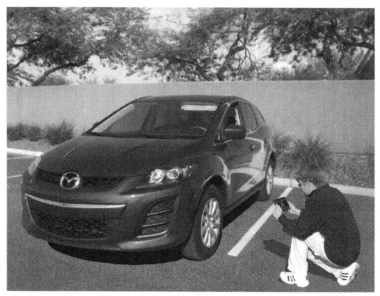

As cameras on smart phones and tablets improve, it becomes increasingly reasonable to do everything with one device. Photo courtesy of CDMdata.

Some of the veterans who have merchandised vehicles for several years or more will resist any change toward following a recorded process. If the task required of them is the same, and they are always available to do it, then their argument is sound. Repeated tasks from experienced veterans don't require this kind of intrusion. You wouldn't expect someone to use a navigation system to get home from work every day.

On the other hand, If you want to change the task frequently or provide others with the ability to complete the task in absence of the veteran, then having the merchandiser respond to processes rather than memorize them makes all the sense in the world.

Chapter 8 Proper Lighting

For those stores selling hundreds of used vehicles per month, there is ample justification for a dedicated facility with controlled lighting. More professional photos not only enhance preference for the vehicle, they enhance preference for the store. I not sure I will ever be able to control enough variables to empirically support the hypothesis that more professional photos can increase average gross profit. However the theory that better photos can not only increase the conversion of VDPs to contacts but also increase average gross is very reasonable.

This inexpensive interior photo booth, allows for greater control of lighting than can be achieved in the open. Photo courtesy of Mobile Inspector by cDemo.

Increased revenue is not the only reason for developing a controlled environment. The sun changes both with the hour of the day and the month of the year. The best place to take photos in the morning may not be any good at all in the

84

afternoon. The location that provides four hours of optimal lighting in one month may provide only a fraction of that time six months later. When you combine the limitations of lighting with the interruptions caused by weather, it is very difficult to be either fast or efficient with external photography.

Reflect for a moment on the process used at discount photography studios, the kind found in many department stores. The trick to creating a production process that is fast and inexpensive is avoiding setup time. The lighting rarely needs adjustment for any shot required, and the backgrounds change quickly. Replace the human subjects with vehicles –which are far more cooperative – and eliminate the variance in backgrounds, and you have a production process designed for rapid output any hour of any day, regardless of weather or season.

There are some fascinating techniques for minimizing glare for exterior shots. I've enjoyed reading about the process of taking multiple shots with a polar filter and using PhotoShop to pull them together into one superior photo. Frankly, this kind of perfection cannot possibly be cost effective for selling ordinary vehicles. Exotic cars may prove to be an exception, but that market is beyond the scope of this book.

Seasoned professionals know how to position the vehicle relative to the sun, maximizing the opportunity even when the possibilities are limited. Photo courtesy of Dealer Specialties.

Many stores have no choice but to take their photos outside. That doesn't mean you can't provide some control for the lighting. Here are some requirements for establishing the right location:

1. The light is optimal during the time of day when a vehicle merchandiser is available.
2. It is easy to bring vehicles in and out of the location
3. The location is always available during the hours of optimal lighting
   a. It doesn't get used for vehicle overflow
   b. It is clearly posted as a no parking zone
   c. It is not the place where snow gets piled
   d. It does not have adjacent areas where water pools on the ground

The tactical aspects of lighting are beyond the scope of this book and worthy of the many books written on the subject. For the GM or owner principle, the essential aspect of lighting is that it be well thought out as part of the process design. All too often, lighting is something stores try to make the most of only as hindrances to good lighting are discovered during the execution phase.

Chapter 9 Proper Sound

Two things are critical for proper video narration, making sure the narrator can be clearly heard and eliminating any distracting sound.

While many cameras include a microphone directly on the unit, this is generally not ideal. The distance between the mouth of the narrator and the microphone should remain constant. Additionally, speech should be continually aimed directly at the microphone. Lapel microphones are a good option, but care must be taken to make sure the mic stays in place and nothing rubs against it.

When using an iPhone or other smart phone, there are several options. The in-ear headphones that come equipped with a remote mic on the cord can deliver reasonably good audio. Microphones are available that plug directly into the iPhone to essentially become part of the device. This is a good option when using the iPhone purely to record audio, but can present problems when using the device to both capture video and audio.

Handheld microphones are another option. This is another of those devices that looks cool and would be great for recording audio only or for a two-person approach. However, greatest efficiency is achieved when one person operates the device and provides the audio at the same time. This process generally requires a hands-free microphone that can be attached to the operator. As mentioned, the best attachments are on the lapel or hanging from the earbuds.

It is not enough to control the consistency of the narrator's voice entering the microphone, you must do your best to keep other noise out. This is difficult. Everything about cars seems to be noisy. Cars make noise, car repair is noisy, and car selling requires noise. Even when the store appears quiet, there is usually some kind of background noise that will be picked up. Sound control is another reason for dedicating a facility to vehicle merchandising. There are a multitude of systems for mitigating noise once it enters the recording, but dealerships don't have time for that. The best way to control noise for every vehicle video is to keep it from reaching the microphone in the first place.

If you must shoot your video outside, and many stores do, then find a place where the sound problems are minimized during the hours of optimal lighting. With all the lighting constraints mentioned in the previous chapter, this may seem like one burden too many, but good audio is critical. Remember, about 25% of the shoppers seeing your listings are primarily audio learners. They want to hear the message. The photos are interesting, but just don't come together in these shoppers' minds to tell the story.

Chapter 10 Customizing the Process

As pointed out in Chapter 7, simplicity is the mother of speed. One of the challenges faced in vehicle merchandising is fact that the process is going to require modification from time to time. Change is often the enemy of simplicity. Things seem simple when we do them frequently with consistency. So how do we execute change without destroying simplicity?

To find the answer, we must address the question before change is needed. If we know the process will change due to vehicle changes, policy changes, and the discovery of new methods of achieving competitive advantage, then we must build the ability to change into the process. Part of designing a great process requires designing one with the following features relative to change:

1. The process can be changed quickly
2. The vehicle merchandisers can quickly adapt to the change
3. Adaptation to the change appears simple to the vehicle merchandisers
4. Changes impact as few people as possible
5. The operator cannot avoid adoption of the change

This last point is essential. For maximum efficiency, vehicle merchandising is a one-person at a time operation, and that has consequences that must be accounted for. As an example, if two people wash cars together every day, they begin to accept that they must remain on the same page, and that maximum efficiency is achieved when they do things the same way each time that the situation is the same. If those same two people are asked to wash the same cars but to work independently in shifts, each will eventually develop their own process for executing the task. When change is injected, it often impacts one person's process more than the other's. Eventually the processes are not the only things that are different, the outcomes are different too. At that point, changes are routinely rejected. Many people who independently control a process eventually take ownership of it, for better or for worse. They may use that freedom to execute improvements to the process, or they may cut corners, increase risk, or unilaterally diminish output standards.

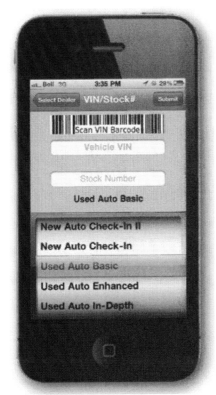

The Mobile Inspector app provides several preprogrammed processes that can be modified for the store.

There is no room for individual expression when it comes to vehicle merchandising. Your photos and videos need to convey your one and only brand image, and they need to convey it in the same way every time. The importance of brand standards across the entire marketing mix has been well documented in a wide variety of books, studies, and articles. You cannot achieve consistent outcomes over a prolonged period involving multiple changes without insisting on a uniform process and insisting that every change be adopted by every vehicle merchandiser.

By building the process into the device used to capture the vehicle merchandising, rather than training it into the vehicle merchandiser, the manager has distant control over the process and changes to it. Taking this back to the GPS comparison, changing the merchandising requirements and the processes can be as simple as changing your navigation system to provide routes based on the least amount of time rather than least distance.

Even the process for how the vehicles will be staged for photos and video must be clear and consistent. Photo courtesy of Mobile Inspector by cDemo.

Without a process built into the device or application, Managers can either inspect the process, inspect the outputs from the process, or accept whatever it is they receive from the process.

Chapter 11 Deciding Who

By now it should be clear how critical the Vehicle Merchandiser function is. Yet this should never be just one person, and for most stores it will not be the sole function of anyone on staff. The work can be tedious for some. Additionally, this is not a desk job; it is physical work with stamina requirements. Finding someone who is willing to do this work and is extremely dependable can be difficult. For some stores this is reason enough to contract out the function. Other dealers recognize how difficult it is to gain a competitive advantage by outsourcing to the same firm that does the same work for your competitor. Rather than try to reach a conclusion regarding the decision to outsource the vehicle merchandising or perform it in-house, we will explore the optimal way to do each, as well as the pros and cons.

Outsource

Outsourcing is fast and easy to get started with just about any provider. One of the downsides to outsourcing is that you may be forced to accept their process and their system. Therefore, don't just look at the outcome as advertised. Look at the system. Does it utilize a process that will expand with you? It might be a great system for producing photos and videos, but does it verify the equipment on the vehicle. Will it give your team the accurate information they need to improve the ratios of appointments to contacts, shown appointments to appointments, and sales to shown appointments plus walk-ins?

Be sure you know how often they are coming to merchandise your vehicles. If it is not every day, then your ability to turn your inventory will not be optimized. If that is an acceptable tradeoff, be sure they are coming on the days you need them most. Chances are, there are a few days of the week with more vehicles arriving for sale and coming out of reconditioning than the other days of the week. Try to sync the scheduling up to your needs rather than the convenience of the vendor. Some services will come to the store every day if need be, and still charge only on a per-vehicle basis.

Be sure you know how the vendor is going to merchandise your vehicles when the person who usually does it is sick, on vacation, or suddenly leaves the firm. Like most entrepreneurs, I have a soft spot for the little firms and have found many small companies in various industries that provide great service. However, you must be certain they can deliver the service you need consistently.

What is the company's policy for poor weather? If the photos are going to be shot outdoors, there must be a known policy for how the pictures will be taken if you are hit with one or more days of prohibitive weather.

In-House

The in-house decision is as much about how many as it is which ones. You must have backup, and you must have a defined process that is simple enough to allow someone to perform the merchandising function even if they are only called upon to do it once every few months. Fortunately the systems are becoming easier. Vendors are beginning to use devices like smart phones and tablets that people are already familiar with, and the best of them require virtually no training. Applications are made to be simple and self explanatory. If the system is as easy to use as Angry Birds or some other popular game app, then you should have no problem finding people who can use it.

CDMdata's Linda Adams convincingly says, "Mobile is the future." Photo Courtesy of CDMdata.

Your core person must be someone who can follow the process and not start figuring out secretive ways to cut corners. If a change in the process is justified, then change the process for everyone performing it. The Vehicle Merchandiser cannot be someone who feels they can pick and choose which parts of the process they want to follow and which they don't. The mission is too critical to act as though these are only pictures, videos, and words on a web page. After all, we are talking about selling vehicles at the very first stage of the sales process. In my view, attitude is the most important characteristic. A willingness to follow the process, particularly if the process is easy to circumvent, may be the most important characteristic.

Next is the ability to work quickly for long periods of time. Vehicles Merchandising must take place every day that new inventory arrives. Getting some of the day's new inventory merchandised and saving the rest for tomorrow is not an option. The optimal deadline for getting vehicles merchandised online is no later than the moment it is available for sale. Where state law allows the practice, it is perfectly legitimate to post inventory still in the pipeline, provided you note the date the vehicle will become available. The volume of inventory to be merchandised will be much higher on some days than others, and your team must be able and willing to step up to that task with speed and accuracy.

 Given a choice between a knowledge of photography and a knowledge of cars, I recommend you choose the latter. Photography is getting easier and easier as technology advances. Vehicles are become more complex. That said, the system should be simple enough for anyone to use. Choose your system to be simple enough for the backups to use, or you will have days when the job just does not get finished and sales are lost.

My brother, Pastor Gary Galbraith, merchandising vehicles with an app on his iPhone. With no training or prior experience, he was able to pick it up quickly.

Because of the wild variability in the amount of merchandising work to do each day, and the need to complete it, you need to have enough capacity to handle the heaviest days and enough flex work related to non-merchandising tasks to fill in the remainder of the schedule. Unless you can obtain extreme flexibility from your vehicle merchandisers, determining what other work they will take on is a critical part of any in-house program.

Getting the vehicles merchandised online must be a priority that is clearly understood across the organization. Various managers will be tempted to elevate the tasks they need done above the task of merchandising vehicles. That cannot be permitted to happen or future sales will suffer.

About the Author

Dennis Galbraith leads Research and Business Intelligence for Dealers at DrivingSales. He is the author of *Sales Integration* and holds an MBA from the University of Southern California.

Through DrivingSales, Dennis delivers research services to dealers and their vendors as well as consulting and training. He has owned two successful companies serving dealers and vendors, Dennis Galbraith Marketing Services and Revenue Guru. Through the 1990's he taught marketing at the graduate and undergraduate level for Embry-Riddle Aeronautical University. Dennis ran the automotive internet division of J.D. Power and Associates until 2006, then managed over $300,000,000 in advertising products as Cars.com's Vice President of Advertising Products and Training.

Dennis taught marketing for NADA Academy and is a frequent speaker at industry events. Dennis and his editorial partner, Lindsey Auguste, can be read regularly on DrivingSales.com.

Made in the USA
Charleston, SC
26 January 2012